Next Time You See a BEE

BY EMILY MORGAN

NSTA Kids
National Science Teachers Association
Arlington, Virginia

National Science Teachers Association

Claire Reinburg, Director
Rachel Ledbetter, Managing Editor
Andrea Silen, Associate Editor
Jennifer Thompson, Associate Editor
Donna Yudkin, Book Acquisitions Manager

ART AND DESIGN
Will Thomas Jr., Director

PRINTING AND PRODUCTION
Catherine Lorrain, Director

NATIONAL SCIENCE TEACHERS ASSOCIATION
David L. Evans, Executive Director

1840 Wilson Blvd., Arlington, VA 22201
www.nsta.org/store
For customer service inquiries, please call 800-277-5300.

Lexile® measure: 940L

NSTA is committed to publishing material that promotes the best in inquiry-based science education. However, conditions of actual use may vary, and the safety procedures and practices described in this book are intended to serve only as a guide. Additional precautionary measures may be required. NSTA and the authors do not warrant or represent that the procedures and practices in this book meet any safety code or standard of federal, state, or local regulations. NSTA and the authors disclaim any liability for personal injury or damage to property arising out of or relating to the use of this book, including any of the recommendations, instructions, or materials contained therein.

Library of Congress Cataloging-in-Publication Data

Names: Morgan, Emily R. (Emily Rachel), 1973- author.
Title: Next time you see a bee / by Emily Morgan.
Description: Arlington, VA : National Science Teachers Association, [2019] |
   Series: Next time you see | Audience: K to grade 3.
Identifiers: LCCN 2018048636 (print) | LCCN 2018051531 (ebook) | ISBN
   9781681406534 (e-book) | ISBN 9781681406510 (print) | ISBN 9781681406527
   (library binding)
Subjects: LCSH: Bees--Juvenile literature. | Pollination by bees--Juvenile
   literature.
Classification: LCC QL565.2 (ebook) | LCC QL565.2 .M6684 2019 (print) | DDC
   595.79/9--dc23
LC record available at *https://lccn.loc.gov/2018048636*

To Clay Bolt for introducing me and countless others to the beauty and importance of our native bees.

"When we try to pick out anything by itself, we find it hitched to everything else in the Universe."

—John Muir

A NOTE TO PARENTS AND TEACHERS

The books in this series are intended to be read with children *after* they have had some experience with the featured objects or phenomena. For example, go outside on a warm, sunny day with your child or students and find a patch of flowers. Watch the bees as they fly from flower to flower. Choose one bee to follow with your eyes, and watch it carefully. Take photos or slow-motion videos of it. Talk with your child or students about what you observe, and share what you wonder. *Why is the bee visiting these flowers? Is there any kind of pattern to the way it moves? What is that yellow stuff sticking to its body?*

After you have had some experiences observing these fascinating insects, read this book together. Take time to pause and share your learnings and wonderings with each other. You will find that new learnings often lead to more questions.

The *Next Time You See* books are not meant to present facts to be memorized. They are written to inspire a sense of wonder about ordinary objects or phenomena and foster a desire to learn more about the natural world. Children might initially be afraid of bees. However, when they learn how important bees are to humans and the planet, their fear will hopefully develop into appreciation. My wish is that after reading this book, you and your child or students feel a sense of wonder the next time you see a bee.

—Emily Morgan

Safety Note: Teachers, be sure to check with your school nurse about bee-sting allergies and how to deal with them before observing bees. Bee allergies are uncommon and usually associated with honeybees. Bees are unlikely to sting while foraging unless you grab them. However, bee allergies can be life-threatening, so it is important to know if any of your students are allergic and take precautions.

Next time you see a bee,
stop and watch it for a while.
Stay still and follow it with
your eyes.

What colors do you
see on its body?
Can you see its wings?
Can you find its eyes?
Can you count its legs?
Listen carefully.
Is it making a sound?
How would you describe
the way the bee moves?
What do you think
it might be doing?

Bees are some of the most important and fascinating insects on Earth. They can be found almost anywhere—from farms to deserts to cities to your own backyard.

The daily activities of these tiny animals affect our lives in a BIG way. Have you ever wondered how such small, common insects can be so important?

Pollination! Bees spend their days flying from flower to flower. As they dart among the blossoms, the insects unknowingly carry out the process of pollination. Pollination allows plants to produce fruit, seeds, and eventually more plants. The remarkable role bees play in pollination makes them vital to our planet.

Bees have no idea how important they are to the plants they visit. The insects travel to flowers simply to gather their food. They eat nectar and pollen produced by the flowers, and they also feed these substances to their young. Nectar is a sweet liquid and pollen is a sticky powder.

If you look near the center of a flower, you can often see pollen. It is usually yellow but can also be white, brown, pink, and many other colors. If you touch the pollen with your finger, you can feel the sticky grains.

Pollen is an extraordinary substance. When the powder is moved from one flower to other flowers of the same kind during the process of pollination, it makes it possible for these flowers to produce fruit or seeds.

Most plants need help moving their pollen from flower to flower. The wind can blow the pollen of certain plants to other flowers. But most flowering plants rely on animals like bees to transport their pollen. These animals are called *pollinators*.

Over time, pollinators and flowers have developed a special relationship in which they depend on each other. Pollinators need flowers for food, and flowers need pollinators to spread their pollen. In addition to bees, several other kinds of animals pollinate plants, including butterflies, moths, wasps, flies, beetles, birds, and bats. But none of these are as prolific a pollinator as the bee.

Bees' bodies are perfect for pollination. Two large compound eyes and three simple eyes help the insects find flowers. Two pairs of wings allow them to fly and hover as they move from flower to flower. Six legs help them perch on or grab hold of a flower. Two antennae let them sense their surroundings. And one exceptional feature that makes them especially good pollinators is that the bodies of most bees are covered with tiny, feathery hairs. Pollen sticks to these hairs and travels with the bees from flower to flower. Some bees even have *pollen baskets* (small, curved surfaces on their back legs) where they can carry the pollen.

Bees pollinate many plants that then bear
things we eat: apples, tomatoes, lemons, limes,
blueberries, cherries, almonds, pumpkins,
watermelons, blackberries, pears, apricots,
peaches, avocados, cucumbers, sunflower seeds ...
the list goes on and on. Next time you enjoy one of
these foods, you can thank bees!

The honeybees we are so familiar with today are not native to North America. Settlers from Europe brought them across the ocean on ships to make honey and beeswax. Most honeybees in North America are *domesticated*. That means beekeepers raise them in hives and have some control over where they go and what they pollinate. Large orchards and farms bring in truckloads of honeybee hives to make their crops produce as much fruit as possible.

There are more than 4,000 species of wild bees in North America that pollinate right alongside honeybees. We call these *native* bees because they are a natural part of North America's ecosystems, and they have been pollinating plants here long before the honeybees arrived. Once you start looking for these insects, you will notice them more and more. You will see their beautiful colors and range of shapes and sizes.

Most native bees nest alone rather than in colonies, so they are sometimes called *solitary* bees. You might see solitary bees flying in and out of holes in a wall, in wood, or in the ground. These holes are where they lay their eggs. Some solitary bees make nests for their eggs using leaves or mud. The insects go back and forth between flowers and the nests, collecting and depositing pollen and nectar for their young to eat when they hatch.

Honeybees are efficient pollinators, but they are unable to pollinate certain plants. Take, for example, the tomato plant. The pollen inside of a tomato flower does not simply fall off as with many other flowers. Instead, the flower has to release the pollen. A bumblebee has a special trick to make this happen—a process called buzz-pollination. The bee unhinges its wings, grabs onto the flower, and buzzes. The vibration of the buzz causes the pollen to burst out of the flower. Isn't that amazing?

If you want to observe bees, find a patch of flowers on a warm, sunny day. Search for bees flying quickly from bloom to bloom. Watch them land on the flowers and put their heads inside to get to the nectar. Look closely to see if you can notice any pollen sticking to their bodies.

Some people get nervous around bees because they are afraid of being stung, but most bees do not sting. While it is true that honeybees can sting, most wild bee species are reluctant to do so, and male bees don't even have stingers! If you give bees enough space, they will not bother you.

The good news is that anyone can help bees! You can make a huge difference for bees—no matter where you live. You can provide food for bees by planting bee-friendly flowers, being sure to keep them pesticide-free.

You can also provide nesting areas for native bees by using paper tubes to build a bee house where they can lay their eggs.

So, the next time you see a bee, remember that as it zips from flower to flower to find food, it is doing something quite extraordinary for those plants and for you! It is unknowingly making it possible for plants to produce fruits and seeds ... many of which are foods you eat. It is sometimes hard to believe that something so small can be so important. But bees are key to keeping our planet and ourselves healthy and nourished. Isn't that remarkable?

ABOUT THE PHOTOS

Central bumblebee
(Clay Bolt)

Common eastern bumblebee
(Clay Bolt)

Black-tailed bumblebee
(Clay Bolt)

Mining bee
(Clay Bolt)

Holding pollen
(Clay Bolt)

Butterfly pollinator
(Shutterstock)

Bird pollinator
(Shutterstock)

Honeybee with pollen baskets
(Clay Bolt)

Long-horned bee
(Clay Bolt)

Long-horned bee covered in pollen
(Clay Bolt)

Various bee species
(Clay Bolt)

Honeybees buzzing around hives
(Shutterstock)

Halictus sweat bee (left) and metallic green bee (right)
(Clay Bolt)

Leafcutter bee carrying leaf to line her nest
(Clay Bolt)

Bee in greenhouse
(Clay Bolt)

Observing bees
(Tom Uhlman)

A group watching bees
(Tom Uhlman)

Rusty patched bumblebee
(Clay Bolt)

Sanderson's bumblebee
(Clay Bolt)

Planting bee-friendly flowers
(Tom Uhlman)

Creating a bee house
(Tom Uhlman)

Mining bee feeding on a flower
(Clay Bolt)

Using the Bumble Bee Watch app
(Tom Uhlman)

Activities to Encourage a Sense of Wonder About bees

- ❖ Help native bees by planting native plants, a food source for the insects, in your yard or schoolyard. You can find out what plants are native to your area by finding your region or entering your zip code on the Xerces Society website (see the Websites section).

- ❖ Be sure not to use pesticides when gardening or growing food.

- ❖ Join the Bumble Bee Watch program, and use its app to photograph, identify, and submit data about bumblebees in your area (see the Websites section).

- ❖ Participate in the Great Sunflower Project by growing lemon queen sunflowers, observing the pollinators, and sharing your observations (see the Websites section).

- ❖ Make or buy a nesting box for native bees.

- ❖ Get a better look at how bees pollinate by using a slow-motion video app on a smartphone or tablet.

Websites

Bumble Bee Watch
www.bumblebeewatch.org

The Great Sunflower Project
www.greatsunflower.org

Pollinator Partnership Guides to Selecting Plants for Pollinators
http://pollinator.org/guides

Xerces Society Pollinator Plant Lists
https://xerces.org/pollinator-conservation/plant-lists

References

Embry, P. 2018. *Our native bees: North America's endangered pollinators and the fight to save them.* Portland, OR: Timber Press.

Moisset, B., and S. Buchmann. 2015. *Bee basics: An introduction to our native bees.* Washington, DC: USDA Pollinator Partnership.

Wilson, J. S., and O. Messinger Carril. 2015. *The bees in your backyard: A guide to North America's bees.* Princeton, NJ: Princeton University Press.